Thanks for you [illegible]

Chris. 1942

Come out and see it sometime!

AYERS ROCK & THE OLGAS

Best wishes

Derek Roff.

Ayers Rock

AYERS ROCK & THE OLGAS

Text & Photography

DEREK ROFF

URE SMITH

Sydney · Auckland · London · New York

ACKNOWLEDGEMENTS

I would like to acknowledge the assistance and interest of Mr C.D. Ollier of the Research School of Pacific Studies, Australian National University, whose comments whilst discussing the geomorphology of the Uluru National Park were a tremendous help.

I must also thank for their assistance in preparing maps used in this book, — Rangers Ian McKinna and Dennis Matthews, of the Territory Parks and Wildlife Commission. Also the personnel of the Territory Parks and Wildlife Commission stationed at Uluru National Park.

(Pages 2/3) The sandhill environment, in many ways, makes a welcome change from the mulga areas. The breeze plays along the crests of the sandhills working the sand into the ripple patterns and causing wind corridors that eventually develop into channels through the sandhills. The dune tops are constantly moving and changing and the types of sandhill vegetation are, in many cases, very different to the plants of the mulga.

(Pages 4/5) These domes are excellent examples of the continuing process of erosion that is called 'off loading'. The steep sides and round tops of this form of spheroidal weathering are the result of millions of years of constant erosion.

Published by Ure Smith, Sydney
a division of Paul Hamlyn Pty Limited
176 South Creek Road, Dee Why West, NSW, Australia 2099
First published 1979

Produced in Australia by the Publisher
Typeset in Australia by G. T. Setters Pty. Limited
Printed by Toppan Printing Co. (Singapore) (Pte) Limited
38 Liu Fang Road, Jurong, Singapore 22

National Library of Australia Cataloguing-in-Publication Data

Roff, Derek.
Ayers Rock and the Olgas.

ISBN 0 7254 0472 8

1. Ayers Rock — Mount Olga National Park, Northern Territory. I. Title.

919.4'29 [1]

CONTENTS

FOREWORD

DEREK Roff has been in charge of the Uluru (Ayers Rock-Mount Olga) National Park since October 1968 and it is fitting that the photographic record he has built up should be supplemented by the information he has accumulated on the flora, fauna and geology, and on the earliest inhabitants, the Aborigines.

It is obvious that the author has developed a genuine love for the area and its people, and that a great deal of painstaking research has been carried out. Many publications relating to the area have appeared over the years. Whether the views expressed in this book are universally acceptable is not important: the richness of its contents, illustrative and narrative, will add to our knowledge and stimulate interest.

W. T. Hare
Director
Territory Parks and
Wildlife Commission

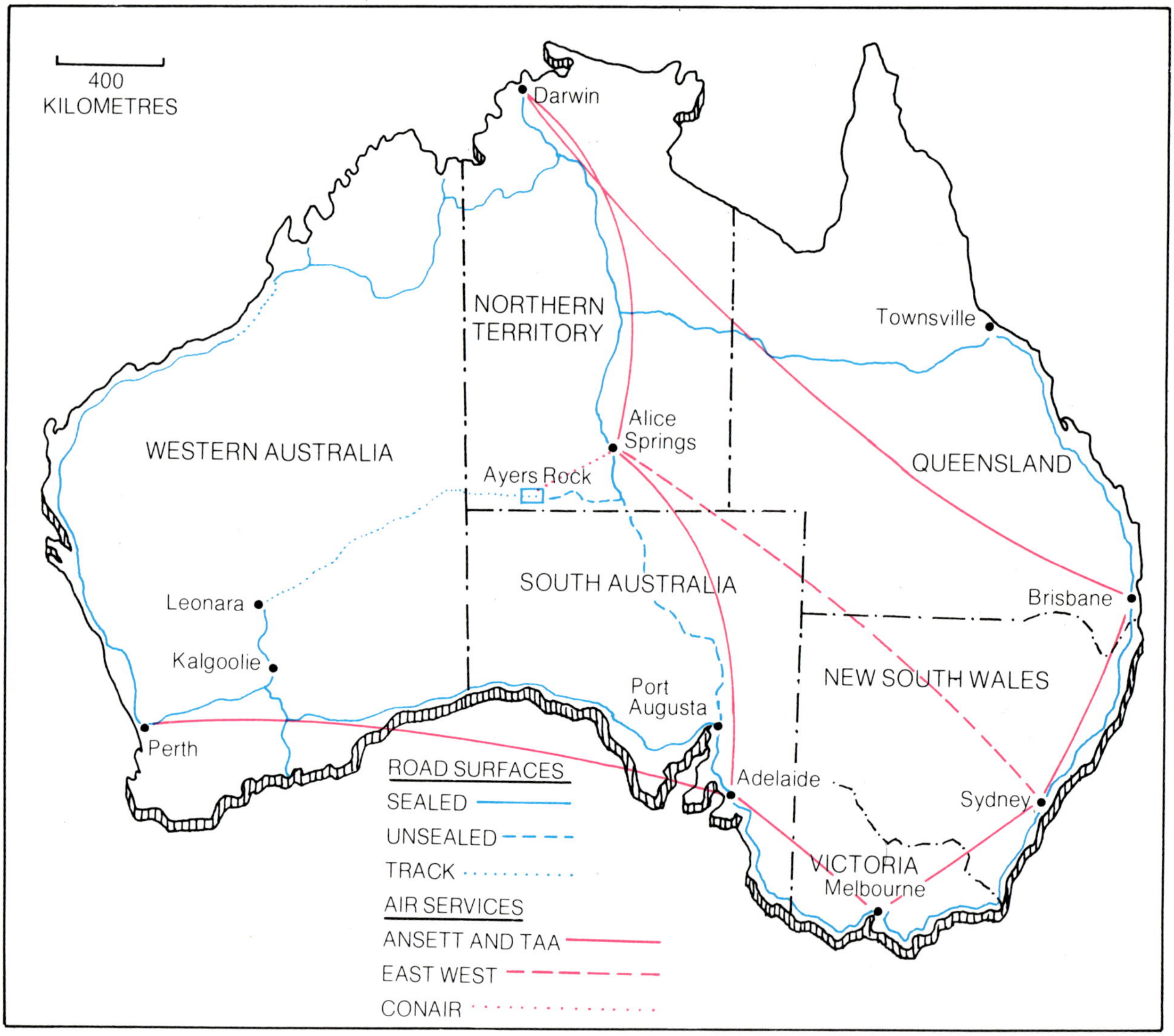

INTRODUCTION

The Uluru (Ayers Rock-Mount Olga) National Park covers an area of 126,132 hectares, and is situated within the arid zone of the Northern Territory of Australia. The area is one of sandy plains and sand dunes interspersed with mulga woodland.

Rainfall is erratic, averaging about 200 mm per annum, which contrasts with the average evaporation rate of 2750 mm per annum. For survival in the desert country all plants and animals have had to become specially adapted and most show a remarkable ability to exist without free water, even when the rains fail for a number of years.

The Aborigines, however, are not able to live in the harsh interior of Australia without free water, but due to their complete involvement with and understanding of nature they have managed to survive over the thousands of years since their ancestors first arrived. Ayers Rock and the Mount Olga group are known to the people of the Yankuntjatjara and Pitjantjatjara tribes as Uluru and Katatjuta respectively. For thousands of years these two inselbergs have been of special significance, and have dominated the lives of the Aborigines of the western deserts. Ayers Rock, situated 478 kilometres south-west of Alice Springs, and the Olgas, 32 kilometres west of Ayers Rock, are attractions that draw many thousands of tourists from Australia and the rest of the world each year.

The desert scene is a fascinating one where, during the past millenia, mountains have risen and been eroded away; populations of plants and animals have interacted with the forming of the land and the environment. Species of flora and fauna have appeared and departed and still, throughout the dry sandplains and within the shadows of the main features of the landscape, life in many forms goes on in constant adjustment to the changing environment.

Derek Roff

THE FORMATION OF AYERS ROCK AND THE OLGAS

Ayers Rock is formed of a sedimentary sandstone known as arkose. When fresh and unweathered, arkose ranges in colour from pale grey to dark grey and green-grey. It is a coarse-grained sandstone and contains a high proportion of quartz and feldspar, with other grains of granite, basalt and clay pellets.

Mount Olga and the surrounding groups of domes make up a formation named Mount Currie conglomerate. This conglomerate contains pebbles and boulders of granite, gneiss and volcanic rock set in a matrix of metamorphosed sandstone containing epidote.

During the Cambrian period 500 to 600 million years ago, part of Central Australia was submerged. An ancient mountain range that had been raised by a geological upheaval known as the Petermann Ranges Orogeny was eroded and sediment deposited in front of the mountains in the sea. Boulder sediments hardened to conglomerate as at Mount Olga; sandy sediments hardened to sandstone as at Ayers Rock.

During a period of tectonic activity, probably late in the Ordovician period (about 450 million years ago) the rocks were folded and uplifted above the sea. At the Olgas the strata are tilted about 20 degrees to the horizontal, but at Ayers Rock they are as steep as 85 degrees, and the near vertical strata are very obvious where the Rock has been weathered into ridges and grooves.

Over hundreds of millions of years enormous quantities of rock have been eroded away from the area, and much of Central Australia has been worn down to a plain. But some of the harder rocks have resisted erosion and now stand out as hills and mountains rising above the great plain. Ayers Rock and the Olgas are typical inselbergs, or island mountains, that rise very abruptly from the plain like islands from the sea. It has been estimated that about 2700 metres of arkose is exposed at Ayers Rock and that the total depth could be over 6000 metres.

Ayers Rock is over 8 kilometres in circumference and is 3.6 kilometres long and 2.4 kilometres wide. It is 348 metres above ground level and 867 metres above sea level. The Rock is eroding by a process of flaking, sometimes called spalling. This flaking is continuous over the whole of the Rock surface and is a weathering process related to rusting. Moisture and air combine with some of the minerals in the rock to produce iron oxides (rust) and clay, causing flakes to fall away. The caves around the Rock, both at the base and higher up the steep sides, are also caused by this form of erosion. Once the flaking has begun the process continues in an upward and inward manner, causing a 'wave-like' shape of the cave. Eventually the overhang collapses through its own weight and forms the piles of rocks found in front of most caves.

The Mount Olga group, west of Ayers Rock, consists of over thirty domes. The highest is Mount Olga itself, which is 546 metres above ground level and 1078 metres above sea level. The circumference of the group is about 30 kilometres. Most domes in the group have extremely steep walls, and narrow gorges and valleys separate adjacent domes.

Much erosion at the Olgas has resulted from a form of 'off-loading', when internal rock stresses have caused large slabs to split away from the main body by cracks parallel to the ground surface. These slabs eventually break down to boulder size and either slide very slowly down the sides of the dome or fall dramatically. Whilst the predominant erosion process at Ayers Rock is flaking, examples of off-loading can be seen at the feature known as Ngaltawata, and at the Climb, Djundi, the Emu leg and several other places.

Around the base of Ayers Rock, where moisture can be retained, there is a zone of fairly dense tree and shrub cover. In the Olgas the loose rock debris in the deep and narrow valleys supports plentiful plant and animal life.

Away from the inselbergs the sandhills and sandplains take over. This sort of country covers large areas of Central Australia and despite the shortage of water, plants and animals have adapted to the environments of the sandhills and mulga savannah woodlands.

The caves of Ayers Rock are formed through moisture causing a chemical reaction with the minerals of the rock surface — a process of hydration that is similar to rusting. Flaking occurs causing a dimple to be formed. The continuing process enlarges the dimple working inwards and upwards shaping the cave into a 'wave pattern'. Overhanging rock eventually collapses through its own weight enlarging the caves more rapidly. Most cave development occurs at ground level where moisture is retained longer and many caves on the high slopes of the Rock suggest long periods of pause as the plains around the Rock have been lowered over millions of years.

(Left) Off-loading erosion at the Olgas, where great slabs of rock have split away the main domes. This process is probably caused by internal pressure and possibly assisted by thermal differences resulting from the pressure. As the process has continued over many years the sides of the domes have become steeper and the tops more rounded. Many of the slabs of rock have fallen dramatically but others can be seen here in the process of moving slowly and gently downwards into the valley.

(Top) Olga conglomerate showing the round boulders of granite, the greenish epidotised granite (symbolic of great pressures on the rock whilst at tremendous depth in the earth's crust) and the grey-black of the basalt, a volcanic flow rock. The conglomerate is welded together in a sandstone matrix.

(Above) Arkose, the material that comprises Ayers Rock, is a sedimentary rock made up of granite, basalt, quartz and feldspar, and many other minerals which appear as trace elements. As can be seen in this picture, small pebbles are compressed together in a matrix of sandstone.

ABORIGINAL SETTLEMENT IN THE AREA

Toby Naninga extracting witchetty grub from acacia root. The witchetty grub is one of the favourite foods of the desert nomads. When the time of year is right the people move to the known areas where large numbers of these grubs are to be found in the roots of shrubs particularly those of *Acacia kempeana* the Witchetty bush. Rich and buttery, the grubs are full of protein.

The first people to inhabit the area were the ancestors of the present day Aborigines. There are two main tribal groups in the Park area today. The Yankuntjatjara are the traditional 'owners' while the Pitjantjatjara have moved in from the Western Desert. The two groups are now interrelated. The Aborigines of Central Australia live in a desert environment where the average rainfall is only 152-203mm per annum. The areas adjacent to the main ranges, the Macdonnells, the Musgraves and the Petermanns are relatively well-watered. The dry spinifex-covered plains and the sandhill country which surround Ayers Rock and Mount Olga also form part of the tribal hunting grounds.

There is a lack of knowledge about the origins of the Aboriginal people. It is generally held that they came to the great southern continent from south-east Asia during a period of low sea level when there was only a narrow strait of water to be crossed. There is no doubt, however, that the Aborigines have been in Australia for more than 40,000 years.

The ritual life, mythology and legends of the Aboriginal people revolve around 'Dreamtime' ancestors, which appeared on what was believed by the Aboriginals to be a flat and featureless earth. The actions and behaviour of these ancestral beings laid down the physical features of the land and also gave the laws to the people. The ancestors were believed to have had the mannerisms of man and the instinct and abilities of animals, trees, fruits, or whatever totem they represented.

Cave paintings found in rock shelters weathered at the base of Ayers Rock and ancient rock engravings in the Olgas, illustrate the legends of the Aboriginal Dreamtime. Representations of the actions of the animal ancestors are repeated many times throughout the caves at the Rock. Legends still play an important role in the everyday life of the Aborigines and they constantly refresh their knowledge of them by singing songs as they pass the features of the landscape which to them, are the complete and truthful evidence of *Tjukurapa* — the Dreamtime, when the world and man began.

Every Aboriginal is related to one or more of the Dreamtime ancestors and from an early age is schooled in the law and ritual of his particular totemic ancestor. This feeling of relationship is extremely strong and enduring. The rituals require certain traditional acts to be performed on special occasions, to ensure that the ancestors are content and that the animal or vegetable form of the ancestor continues to exist and be available for use by their human relations.

Knowledge of traditions is handed down from generation to generation in the form of songs and legends from the Dreamtime. The Aborigines must memorise the laws, as they control every aspect of the world in which they live and it is this knowledge that enables continued existence in the harsh conditions of the Centre.

In common with other inhabitants of the arid area, the Aborigines adapted to the harsh conditions. Over many thousands of years they developed a knowledge of the habits of the animal world and of the food and medicinal values of the plantlife, and achieved the ability to live as one with nature. In the Aborigines' concept of life in the desert the protection of the individual is less important than the protection of the family group. When sickness strikes, they cure themselves by using plants and herbs.

Knowledge of available water supplies, as waterholes or soakages or obtainable from certain plants, was essential to the nomadic desert dwellers. The geography of the desert waterholes was passed from one generation to the next in ritual songs; obviously the care of water supplies was of particular importance.

The nomads would wander from waterhole to waterhole depending on the rains and food supplies. Holes and soaks were periodically cleaned and protected from animals and evaporation by covering with branches, leaves and sometimes flat stones. The Aborigines believe that all permanent waterholes are guarded by fearsome water serpents named *Wanambi*, which ensure that the water is protected from strangers who could damage it. Most water supplies are central to important rituals and consequently assume sacred significance. It is for this reason that many European explorers were attacked at waterholes, rather than the Aborigines' fear that the water supplies would be damaged.

Basically the Aborigines practised pure conservation. Restrictions on hunting and eating certain animals and plants at particular times of the year and strict control of hunting near waterholes point to their efforts to conserve their resources of animal and vegetable life.

(Above) Ranger Toby Naninga inspecting a native plum bush. Known to the Aborigines as *kupata* the shrub is a member of the sandalwood family, and has the scientific name *Santalum lanceolatum*. As can be seen in the picture the fruits, a popular food, are about the size of a grape.

(Below) In the desert country surrounding the national park, hunting is still carried out and despite the availability of modern weapons this man of the Yankuntjatjara is still dependent on his knowledge of the 'dreamtime' for his drink of water.

In extremely dry seasons many waterholes would fail and the desert people would be hard pressed to obtain adequate supplies. It was then that an intimate knowledge of plantlife was of paramount importance. A small amount of moisture could be obtained by chewing succulent plants such as the *Parakeelya* and the *Portulacas*. Dewy mornings enabled moisture to be collected from some desert shrubs such as *Thryptomene maisonneuvii* and used to make a sweet, sugary-tasting drink. A number of trees in the region hold moisture in their root systems and when these are cut water drips from the porous fibres. In some instances quite an appreciable amount of fluid can be obtained. Trees that can be used in this way include the Desert Kurrajong which is a most important dry country tree as it provided not only water but food from its tubers and wood for artifacts. Eucalypts and some of the *Hakea* group of trees are also a source of water in bad times. Along creeks and in some soakages native frogs of the waterholding species such as the *Cyclorana* can be found, their presence given away by cracks in the hard, dry ground; when squeezed, these frogs exude water

As no animals were domesticated by the Australian Aborigines or seed plants cultivated, the Aborigines remained hunters and gatherers. They live right up to the twentieth century in a country free from ferocious animals of the kind that would threaten them. As a result of this situation they did not develop the more sophisticated weapons such as the heavy, iron-bladed spears used by Africans for protection against predators.

In order to hunt, gather and prepare foodstuffs and make artifacts, the Aborigines used a range of naturally available materials. Stones served to grind seeds and crush fruits, and also for making knives and scrapers. Spears were made from a type of vine, *Pandorea doratoxylon*, which grows profusely in the Olga gorges and valleys. Heavy, hardwood boomerangs and spearthrowers were cut from desert Mulga trees, while light shields and carrying bowls were shaped from the trunks of the softwood Bean tree. Animal tendons and sinews were used to bind barbs on to spears, and a vegetable adhesive obtained from spinifex grass was used to repair artifacts and to affix stone flakes to wooden handles for use as chisels and scraping tools. Spinifex gum was also used to haft stone knives. A good supply of this useful material was carried by most Aborigines when travelling across the desert country.

Among their main weapons is the spearthrower, which is used in a multiplicity of ways, as a firemaking tool, a grinding bowl, a carrying bowl, or as a chisel or scraper. Its main use is to enable the spear to be thrown further and more accurately. Stone tools included grinders, hammers and edge-ground axes, all of which were specially shaped for appropriate use. Large heavy grindstones were carried many kilometres and left on camp-sites which were constantly revisited. Many of these tools can still be found in the Park. (It should be noted that it is illegal to remove these or any other objects or plants.) The most common stone tool found today is a small flaked blade called by the local Aborigines *kadidi*, which means teeth. This name has its origin in a Dreamtime myth. These 'chipstones' are carefully shaped and show, in many instances, delicate serrations made by striking the edge with a small hammer-stone or sometimes by the maker prising off small chips with his teeth. The chipping forms a fine sawtooth edge. This small tool was used for scraping sinews from animals, shaping and incising patterns on wooden weapons and utensils, and for making ritual objects.

With these few tools and weapons, the Aborigines were able to survive in the desert country. During harsh periods they were dependent on a knowledge of the country and the animals and plants which shared their tribal lands.

The Aborigines developed an outstanding ability to recognise and to follow animal tracks of all kinds and were able to merge into the landscape itself when stalking a kangaroo or euro. As well as providing food, animals were a source of skins, tendons, feathers, hair, bones and sinews that were used for making artifacts and objects of personal adornment for both ritual and secular use.

The traditional tools and artifacts of the Aborigines are now in great demand as souvenirs by visiting tourists. Here, another of the main elders of the park, Pompey Douglas, is decorating a spear. The spears are made from a vinelike shrub that grows in the Olgas. The Aboriginal name for the spear is *kulata*.

Important in the Aboriginal diet was meat which was a source of protein. This was obtained from kangaroos, euros, wallabies, dingoes, possums and echidnas; from reptiles such as non-venomous snakes, lizards and pythons; from birds including emus, pigeons, bustards, budgerigars and finches; and from insects, in particular witchetty grubs. Fish from the rivers of the Centre were a rare delicacy. In later years the rabbit was introduced and became a main food animal.

Plant foods were used to supply bulk to the diet. The Aborigines had to know where and at what time of the year grass seeds were ready for harvesting; the places where the sweet yams could be gathered; and when and where the succulent desert fruits such as native plums (*Santalum lanceolatum*), rock figs (*Ficus platypoda*) and quandongs (*Santalum acuminatum*) could be found. The women of the family groups would be kept busy gathering grass seeds, yams, tubers, some roots and young shoots, in addition to green plants like the *Parakeelya* and *Portulaca*. The latter succulents were either eaten raw or cooked between hot stones. Minute grass seeds and *Portulaca* seeds were ground and mixed to a paste that was consumed raw or cooked in a form of damper. Fruits such as native peaches, plums, figs and native tomatoes were consumed raw. Figs and native tomatoes were also dried, crushed and mixed to a paste and eaten. To protect native peaches or quandongs from emus and other birds and animals, the Aborigines constructed catching tables beneath the trees. Later the fruits were gathered and used by passing groups.

Another source of food was the insect galls found on some *Acacia* trees; also the flowers of plants like *Grevillea eristachya* and *Brachysema chambersii* could be chewed for their nectar. This was one of the few sources of sugar available to the Aborigines of this desert region. Honey also was obtained from the honeyant ahd the hive or 'honeybag' of the native bee.

(Far left) Brachysema chambersii, an interesting desert plant that appears to grow upside down! The flowers appear at ground level whilst the grasslike leaves grow above. The red flowers contain a nectar that the Aborigines use as a form of sugar by sucking the base of the flowers.

(Left and below) Grevillea Eristachya, one of the many foodplants used by the desert nomads. From the large yellow flowers a rich nectar that tastes similar to honey is sucked. This is a highly prized delicacy especially by the children and is particularly important because of its high sugar content.

EUROPEAN EXPLORATION

Ngoru, known to Europeans as 'the brain' because of its shape. This cave at Ayers Rock symbolises the camp of the Elders of the Dreamtime.

The first white man to see Ayers Rock and Mount Olga was the explorer, Ernest Giles. In October 1872 Giles saw the mountain group which he named the Olgas (after Queen Olga of Spain) when he was north of Lake Amadeus, a large salt lake approximately 144 kilometres long and 16 kilometres wide. Lake Amadeus, also named by Giles (after Philip of Spain) and meaning 'the loved one of God', is 40 kilometres north of Ayers Rock.

Giles endeavoured to cross the lake but, being unsuccessful, determined to return the following year. In 1873, however, the Deputy Surveyor General of South Australia, William Christie Gosse, commencing an exploration north of Alice Springs out past Mount Wedge, followed Giles's 1872 waterholes and, skirting to the east of Lake Amadeus, became the first white man to reach the Rock which he named Ayers after Sir Henry Ayers, the Premier of South Australia.

Gosse, accompanied by an Afghan camel driver named Khamran, arrived at the Rock on 19 July 1873 and, the following day, the two of them climbed the Rock. In September 1873 Giles finally reached the Olgas.

The first scientific visits were made by the Central Australian Exploring Expedition led by William Tietkins, who had previously been second in command to Ernest Giles for a number of trips. Tietkins brought his party to the area in 1889. A few years later, one of the most important scientific parties to travel through the region arrived — the Horn Expedition to Central Australia in 1896. This party under the leadership of Sir Baldwin Spencer made some of the first animal collections in the area.

In 1903 H. Basedow led an expedition to the area which was mainly concerned with prospecting and geology. Basedow made geological observations of Ayers Rock, Mount Olga and Mount Connor.

Mount Olga rises 546 metres above the plains, and is one of over thirty domes that make up the formation known as 'The Olgas'. Their Aboriginal name is Katatjuta meaning 'many heads' and they are places of legend and rituals.

THE IMPACT OF MAN ON THE ENVIRONMENT

The feral cat is probably one of the greatest dangers to the native mammals that has appeared in Australia for many thousands of years. Often thought to have resulted from the dumping of unwanted pets, it is not really known how or when they first appeared in the country. If they were in fact brought to Australia by Europeans they have extended their range extremely quickly and successfully. They can be found in all habitats, even the most remote and driest parts of the desert.

Even though the Aborigines had adapted to their environment remarkably well, they still exerted great pressures on the ecology. The use of fire in hunting caused considerable sections of the country to be burnt out. Over a period of time this burning resulted in a gradual transition from mulga scrub to grassland. The mulga tree cannot withstand fire; it has thin bark and the sap boils quickly and the tree dies. As eucalypts and casuarinas have relatively thicker bark they are more able to resist the effects of fires other than the occasional 'hot' fires which sweep through extremely heavily vegetated areas where the understorey growth is thick and dry. Over the burnt out stands of mulga, spinifex (*Triodia*) spread rapidly and, over a period, large tracts of the scrub environment became covered in spinifex.

Another pressure on the ecology of the area came from the dingo. It is believed that the first Aboriginal people in Australia eventually made their way to Tasmania, but as the dingo does not appear to have crossed Bass Strait, it is presumed that it was brought in by a later group of Aborigines, a second wave. Dingoes must have made a great impact on the native fauna. They are extremely efficient hunters and killers and would have competed very successfully with the thylacine, or Tasmanian tiger, that would have been the largest native carnivore of that period. The presence on the Australian mainland of the thylacine is evidenced by fossil remains and recently discovered cave paintings in Arnhem Land appear to be good representations of this animal.

Over the thousands of years since the first appearance of the dingo, it appears to have stabilised its position and achieved a good balance with native fauna. With European settlement of Australia came other animals which have not, as yet, achieved this balance. The animals that pose very definite threats to native fauna are the cat, fox, rabbit, mouse and camel. They endanger the native fauna because they have extended their range and are either successful predators or very competitive grazers or seed eaters.

Cats are probably the most dangerous force with which the native fauna have had to contend. Breeding twice a year with large litters, cats increase their population extremely quickly. They have been able to adapt to the dry climate and, in fact, are well able to subsist on an almost water-free diet in much the same way as the mulgara, a native marsupial mouse. The fox is also a predator that threatens native animals, particularly the smaller marsupials. Foxes do not, however, increase as rapidly as cats.

The rabbit is well known as an Australian pest that destroys quite substantial areas of ground cover by eating the roots of plants. Within the park area, the rabbit may have been responsible for the disappearance of certain animals such as the rat kangaroo (*Bettongia leseuri*), the bilby (*Macrotis lagotis*) and the hare-wallaby (*Lagorchestes hirsutus*) that most definitely were, at one time, resident in the area. (Their presence is evidenced by skeletal remains.) Whether or not their disappearance can be attributed to the rabbit, the rabbit remains a pest.

The housemouse (*Mus musculus*) has very definitely extended its sphere of influence: in fact it has very quickly moved into all environments. During good seasons, the mouse population explodes and houses, motels and camping grounds associated with the park have been completely inundated by plagues of mice. They are never as well received as the native hopping mouse (*Notomys alexis*), a very attractive little animal which also periodically produces spectacular population increases.

The camel, originally introduced into the desert as a beast of burden to assist in the exploration of the arid zones, most definitely played a very important role in opening up the country and, indeed, in the European discovery of Ayers Rock and Mount Olga. On the completion of many exploring trips, camels were released or, in some cases, escaped. They bred successfully throughout the desert regions and today there are hundreds in the country surrounding the Uluru National Park.

All introduced animals have affected the native flora and fauna to some extent, but it seems that if the various habitats of the flora and fauna are not destroyed the native species will continue to survive. The preservation of these habitats is one of the main duties of a national park authority and is the reason behind the rules and regulations governing the park.

It is man himself who poses the greatest threat to the park. The tremendous increase in visitors since the park was established in 1958, has caused stresses on the natural environment. The thousands of people who walk around the Rock, naturally cause pathways to appear and these pathways are susceptible to scouring and rapid erosion when the rains come and the water flows with magnificent force down the sides of the Rock. The scours continue to increase in length and breadth as the

Adapted for rapid bipedal movement in the same manner as kangaroos, hopping mice *(Notomys alexis)* are rodents and not marsupials. They are subject to great population fluctuations and numbers increase and decrease extremely suddenly. Little is known about them except that they live in deep, complex burrows and avoid heat stress by remaining below ground during the day. Like the majority of desert fauna they excrete waste nitrogen as highly concentrated urine and are well able to exist in times of drought without free water.

years go by and constitute a problem for the park management. The natural way in which the water was dispersed from around the base of the Rock was in a form of sheet flooding, when water to a depth of 15-20 cm gently flowed over the ground surface. There must have been some sections of scouring, but generally, it seems as if the movement of water was a passive one. Now, with roads and footpaths, many obstructions to natural water flow have been caused and the water, in many cases, follows these roads and paths, thereby depriving some areas of water and over-watering others. In the dry periods, there are now some places with almost no vegetation whilst other spots are too heavily vegetated and provide suitable areas for exotic weeds to achieve a 'foothold' in the park. Nature will eventually resolve the situation and, now that management authorities are becoming much more knowledgeable on arid zone ecology, problems are being recognised, very often before they become serious.

Another effect that the thousands of visitors have on the park is the slow erosion of the cave paintings due to the dust thrown up as the tourist parties visit the galleries. Visitors are also still touching and rubbing the paintings in order to see 'if it will come off'. However, Ranger-conducted tours are combating this problem by making visitors more aware of the beauty and interest of the art.

However, in many ways the Uluru National Park is fortunate. Although many people visit the area, and by their very numbers place pressures on the sections in the immediate vicinity of Ayers Rock and, to a much lesser extent, Mount Olga, the main area of the park, which comprises the sandhills, plains and mulga wilderness, is still practically unaffected by these pressures. The fact, also, that the majority of the fauna is nocturnal and cryptic, ensures that there is no major interference with their life. There are very definite reasons for confidence in the future of the habitat conservation within the Uluru National Park.

The dingo, believed to have been brought to Australia by the Aborigines over ten thousand years ago, has become the desert's top predator. It may once have been responsible for the disappearance of some native animals, but has now achieved an ecological balance with the native fauna.

THE DRY AND WET SEASONS

(Right) Kandju Gorge Waterfall, at Ayers Rock. When the rain comes tremendous flows of water surge over 100 metres down the sides of the Rock. At the base of the waterfalls are large 'plunge' pools and from these pools the water used to gently flood out over the surrounding plain. The many footpaths, tracks and roads at the base of the rock have now developed into watercourses, and the water from the pools now drains out along these paths and tracks.

The climate of the park is classified as arid. During the summer months, from November to March, skies are cloudy and temperatures are high. Moist air from the tropics causes thunderstorm activity. During the winter months the skies are normally clear, the days are warm and the nights are very cool. Indeed, during winter, from April to October, many frosts occur and on occasions the temperature drops to below zero.

The major problem throughout the Central Australian region is lack of water. The average rainfall is between 150 to 250 mm whilst the average rate of evaporation at Ayers Rock is 2750 mm per annum. The rainfall at Ayers Rock is uncertain. Normally, there is some rain in November and February, as a result of the monsoonal activity in the north of the continent. Around July and August the southerly winter rains that extend northwards from South Australia and into the south of the Northern Territory sometimes bring rain to the region. In some years, there are no summer rains in the Ayers Rock area, in other years the winter rains do not appear. It is not uncommon for there to be no rain at all for a number of years. In periods like these, the region completely dries out and the grasses break up and blow away. Some plants lose all sign of top growth and exist only under the soil surface in their root systems. Others die off completely, leaving their seeds lying dormant in the soil, awaiting the coming of rain. And others are able to retain moisture in their leaves or root systems and await the coming of the wet. The area then approaches the accepted ideal of a desert — red sand, as far as the eye can see, interspersed with patches of dried out grasslands and mulga flats.

In the mulga areas, growth beneath the parched, almost leafless tree cover is practically non-existent. The soil in the mulga sections becomes baked hard and cracks appear in the surface.

The larger animals, such as the kangaroo leave the area and the euros keep to the cool gorges and caves where they are able to retain body moisture. The smaller marsupials and rodents stay in their burrows where they aestivate in warm, humid conditions which enable them to avoid undue loss of body moisture.

Desert mammals are extremely well adapted to live in arid conditions. Most urinate in a concentrated form, thereby cutting down water-loss, and they are able to exist on metabolic water obtained from their foods. Many of the desert animals, particularly the euro and the mulgara, do not appear to require free water at all.

Reptiles continue to be active during drought periods in the mornings and evenings. They avoid the overpowering heat of the day, as do the birds. Birds have a body temperature of 41°C and do not experience heat stress until the ambient temperature exceeds this. When this occurs, they seek the shade beneath the trees and shrubs and wait out the hot part of the day panting in an effort to remain cool. Needless to say, during long periods of excessive temperatures in the region of 45°C, many birds die throughout the area. Budgerigars and zebra finches sometimes experience a mortality of up to 90 per cent.

At times of drought, the desert becomes silent. Every living thing, plant, animal or human, awaits the coming of rain. Eventually, the breeze takes on a moistness and becomes stronger. Clouds begin to develop on the west and northwest horizons. Animal activity commences. Insects begin to hatch, and centipedes, scorpions and beetles appear from their deep holes. Ants become extremely busy storing or moving their seed supplies and eventually, large, beautiful drops of rain begin to fall.

The Central Australia rains come during two periods, the summer rains usually around November and February and the winter rains of July and August. The summer rains are of particular importance to the trees and the grasses. Young tree life bursts from the soil and rapidly throws down deep, water-seeking roots. These roots extend deep into the sands to tap the available moisture. In addition to the tap roots, many varieties of trees and shrubs send roots considerable distances just under the surface of the ground so as to gather the maximum benefit from the lighter showers of rain that fall, especially during the drier periods.

Both the sandhills and the mulga stands change almost overnight with the coming of the winter rains. Then the flowers appear in a magnificent array. Perhaps one of the most attractive is the Parakeelya species (genus *Calandrinia balonensis, polyandra* and *remota*), small succulents with showy pink and purple flowers. Parakeelya grows throughout the mulga and the sand dunes and is truly a plant of the desert. The acacias flower profusely, whilst the ephemeral flora grow rapidly, throwing out their blooms for a short period, then forming and dropping their seed ready for the next time. Their work done, the plants slowly die and disappear.

On the sandhills, in addition to the Grevilleas, the Thyrptomenes, Rattlepods, Lobelias, Leschanaultias, Scaevolas and the many pea flowers show out in wonderful array. Within the mulgas is the realm of the daisies, and here are the extensive displays of Helipterum species, the *Helichrysums* and the *Waitzia*. Also in the mulga and adjacent areas are the magnificent 'Pussycat tails' or Ptilotus species. Outstanding among these are *exaltatus* and *macrocephalus*, which are mauve and green respectively. The Goodenia family is well represented as are the Solanum group known as Native tomatoes, a number of the species being edible. The visitor should, however, be wary of trying native foodplants as these are not edible at all times. The Aborigines have a far greater knowledge in this use of these plants and are able to use them quite safely.

The rains bring on the insect hatches to pollinate the flowers and the birds, reptiles and mammals all begin to breed. The timing of birth is important; each animal must breed so as to be able to take advantage of the availability of its food species and so the insect eaters must commence their family so as to have insects for the food of the young. The Masked Woodswallow (*Artamus personatus*) is one of the first birds to begin nesting. At the first sign of a cloud it has been said the Woodswallow picks up a twig. At this time, there is great activity within the area. Birds frantically work constructing their nests, the eggs are quickly laid and brooding commences. The distribution of work between the two sexes would make an enthralling study.

The rain falling on the Rock fills the waterholes and a myriad water animals appear. The Shield Shrimps (*Triops australiensis*) — fabulous creatures of a primitive form that have existed on the Rock for possibly 150 million years — appear in the pools. These animals live on the tiny microscopic plants and animals such as waterfleas in the waterholes. The Fairy Shrimp is also in the pools. Often mistaken for a tiny fish, it fascinates many visitors. Both the Shield and the Fairy Shrimps are able to reproduce by parthenogenesis, which means that their eggs to not need fertilisation by the male. As the first rains fill the pools, eggs that have remained dormant in the sands over the longest period of drought and in temperatures ranging from below freezing to heat in excess of 55°C hatch, and the shrimps begin to build up their population. The first hatch is predominantly female and on maturity they immediately lay eggs that hatch once more into mainly members of the female sex. A few males do appear and these fertilise the eggs of the remaining breeders. It is these fertilised eggs that require extreme periods of desiccation before they are able to germinate, thereby ensuring that brief rainfalls do not cause all eggs to hatch out leaving the animals at the mercy of unpredictable weather.

The dry region frogs come out of their deep holes at the beginning of the rains. These frogs have specially adapted rear feet, shaped much like a spade, to enable them to dig down perhaps 90-100 centimetres where, for most part of the year, having absorbed water into their bodies, they aestivate in humid cells that keep a temperature of about 40°C. When the frogs come out, the waterholes and creeks are noisy with their calls as they find mates and lay their spawn on the edges of the water and in grass or shrubs overhanging the water. Eventually this spawn hatches into tadpoles that are food for many of the desert's inhabitants, or that attract visiting bird species such as the Straw-necked Ibis (*Threskiornis spinicollis*), the White-faced Heron (*Ardea novaehollandiae*), the White-necked Heron (*Ardea pacifica*) and the Egrets (*Egretta alba* and *E. garzetta*) in addition to a number of ducks, dotterels and sandpipers. These are all birds of more equable climes that, in their nomadic or migratory journeys, pass through the Uluru National Park region.

The breeding and life within the waterholes is a frantic affair. Each animal has to complete its lifespan and ensure continuation of its species whilst the water is there. As the pools dry out, the tadpoles and shrimps are forced into the deeper sections eventually to perish, dry out and be blown away by the dry, hot winds of the Centre.

Reptiles also commence their breeding with the rainy period. Many reptiles lay eggs and one of the requirements of reptile eggs is moistness in the sands. If the eggs are permitted to dry out, they do not hatch.

The mammals, such as the kangaroo and the euro, are able to give birth immediately weather conditions are right for them. The tiny animal, usually just over one centimetre in length, finds its way through the mother's fur to the pouch where it will remain fastened to a teat for about six months. Eventually it begins grazing but still returns to the pouch until its mother evicts it when it reaches a considerable size. The larger marsupials are able to mate immediately after a birth and this insures their survival. If the first young one dies, the mother is able to produce again in a matter of days. If the first youngster survives, the unborn embryo is eventually passed out of the mother's body.

The smaller marsupials, such as the Mulgara and the Red-eared Antechinus, do not have a real pouch but an enlarged fold of skin. When these animals give birth, the young ones fix themselves securely to a teat within the fold of skin. Tiny, pink and hairless, they slowly grow on the teat until fur develops, their eyes open and they begin to make very guarded sorties into the outside world. They become very adventurous and leap about attacking each other, and beetles or moths. These tiny representatives of the marsupials are engaging creatures.

As all these species of animal and bird life are growing in their mothers' pouches or in their nests, the predators have commenced their part in the cycle of life. The dingo has given birth to its litter in the old rabbit warrens or beneath the boulders at the Rock or the Olgas. The fox has its family safe in the den, and the Wedgetail eagle and the other birds of prey are laying their eggs, timing them so that when they hatch there will be sufficient food available for their young ones.

The young animals grow and take their places in the passing parade. The sun begins to shine with increased intensity, conditions become humid, the surface water evaporates and the country gradually dries up. Life once more slows down as the animals seek their resting places, protected by the insulating rocks or sands, and wait out the time of the coming of the rains.

When this waterhole at Kandju Gorge, Ayers Rock, is full there would be few more beautiful places. The water is alive with tadpoles, frogs, caddis larvae and dragonflies that constantly hawk over the water surface. Normal cool conditions make this gorge one of the Rock's most attractive areas.

(Below) Floodout from Maggie Springs at Ayers Rock. As more water flows out of Maggie Springs than from any other part of the rock, the vegetation in this particular area is more prolific and varied than anywhere else. High grasses, interesting flowers and shrubs provide a suitable environment for many animals. The echidna particularly favours this section of the Rock due to the long periods of cool and moist conditions.

(Above) The Maggie Springs watersource above Maggie Springs at Ayers Rock where the rain catchment area extends over 500 hectares. All the water falling on this section of rock gathers tremendous momentum and surges down the rock to explode into Maggie Springs.

(Right) Maggie Springs, a beautiful waterhole at Ayers Rock, is almost permanent and is the most important water for a considerable distance in the surrounding desert. Maggie Springs, known to the Aborigines as Mutitjula, plays an important part in the rituals and legends of the Rock. Due to this ritual importance there is a necessity to protect the water and swimming is not permitted.

(Above) After rain, many flowing watercourses appear and some continue running for many days after the rain has ceased. The flowing watercourses allied with the sounds of the dry country frogs make the Olgas a magic place in the wet.

(Right) After rains large waterholes such as this one at Olga Gorge are to be found throughout the Olgas. There are no permanent waterholes in the Olgas but some of the pools take a long time to dry up. Others, however, disappear almost overnight. It is important that intending hikers check with park rangers as to water availability.

(Left) When the rain comes the type of erosion to be found on Ayers Rock causes a great number of waterholes such as this one at Little Rock. Many are extremely shallow but others are quite deep and many water animals such as Shield and Fairy Shrimps live out their life cycles before the pools dry out.

AYERS ROCK

THE CHANGING COLOUR OF THE ROCK

Ayers Rock and the wilderness that surrounds it attract many people, such as naturalists, photographers and artists. But the majority of park visitors arrive on coach or air package tours with the main ambition to see, as promised in the travel brochures, the Rock change colour. These phenomena is advertised in such a way as to appear almost supernatural and, indeed, many visitors believe that by standing in one position for half an hour they will see the Rock change into many different colours. This is not the way to view the changing colours of the Rock as the colour depends on many factors, such as distance, weather conditions, quality of sunlight and time of day.

By spending a full day of twelve hours on the crest of a sand dune, one will enjoy a wonderful experience. Through the day, the Rock puts on its full show and changes from black, in silhouette at daybreak, through deep purple and blue to brown to warm brown red, then to orange and fiery red at sundown, cooling once more to brown, mauve and then quietly merging into the shadows of nightfull.

Visitors will probably be spellbound and reluctant to leave the sandhill; maybe then they will be rewarded by yet another thrill, when the moon rises over the Rock.

The popular viewing periods at the Rock are sunrise and sunset. Both these times are spectacular, weather permitting. The deep intense reds which are familiar to everyone are the result of the sun's rays striking the rock at a low trajectory and reflecting from the surface of the rock which is coated by iron oxides. The day-to-day colour of the rock is a light brown.

Depending on weather conditions, the time of day and the distance from which it is viewed, Ayers Rock can be seen in many guises. These differing moods of the Rock show how it is able to hold even the most casual observer spellbound. One can appreciate the feelings of the desert nomads as they approached this dominant feature of their world knowing that here was water — life to the people of the desert.

THE CLIMB

Another great tourist attraction is the challenge of climbing the world's biggest rock, a challenge that should not be underestimated. The young and the old, the fit and the infirm, all attempt the Climb. There have been one-legged men to the top. The oldest man to climb the Rock was eighty-nine and the oldest lady eighty-two. One young man with a broken leg in a cast went up and down the Rock on his lower anatomy. Having regard to the rough texture of the rock, this was really answering the challenge.

No matter what attracts people to the Ayers Rock and Mount Olga region, they all enjoy themselves and feel that the Rock has produced what it has promised. The fact that people return to the area year after year must prove its attraction.

We are all aware that, to the Aboriginal people, Ayers Rock is an important place of the Dreamtime and is to them sacred. It is now very evident that to all the people of Australia the Rock is a tremendous symbol of their heritage.

(Below) Every day of the year sees a gathering of people at the sand dune known as 'Sunset Strip'. Whatever the conditions the Rock will show one of its guises but a vivid red sunset does not occur every day. If one is fortunate enough to see the Rock turn this brilliant colour, one feels richer for the experience.

(Right) Covering a distance of 1.6 kilometres and rising 348 metres above the surrounding plains, the Climb at Ayers Rock throws a challenge to park visitors. Thousands of people make the effort to climb the Rock and a large number are successful. Over the years there have, unfortunately, been accidents caused by falls and a number of persons have suffered heart attacks so intending climbers should ensure they fully understand the risks if they are not physically fit. They should also stay on the authorised climbing route where they will be reasonably safe.

Thirty-two kilometres west of the Rock lie the Olgas and from these domes Ayers Rock can be seen dominating the surrounding plains and sandhills.

ROCK PAINTINGS

Throughout the caves of Ayers Rock, under and behind boulders scattered around the base of the Rock, are many hundreds of cave paintings that depict the lives, the myths and the legends of the Aboriginal people. The exact age of the Ayers Rock cave paintings is not known but the most accurate guide is a few examples of the art that were photographed and copied by members of the Horn Expedition to Central Australia, led by Sir Baldwin Spencer in 1896. These can only be used to estimate the age when other factors are also taken into consideration, such as the degree of protection from wind, rain and sunshine; the dampness of the cave area and the possible effect of windblown sands. No doubt there are many other factors that should also be considered. Even though no definite estimate can be given on the question of antiquity, there is no doubt that the walls of the caves have been the canvas of many generations of Aboriginal artists.

The colours used in these paintings are red, yellow, white and black; red and yellow are obtained from ochré, white from ashes, and charcoal provides the black. The process of mixing the pigments is a simple one in which the raw material is ground fine and then mixed with a small quantity of water. Considering the simplicity of the process, it is surprising that the paintings have lasted so long.

The Aborigines made the paintings by applying the ochres with the fingers, whilst the more detailed or finer work, and in many cases the outlining of the subject, was carried out with the use of a twig of which the end had been frayed to make a small brush.

Many visitors to the park are surprised at the simplicity of the designs when they see the paintings for the first time. Certainly the majority of the paintings are simple and many are, of course, extremely abstract and symbolic. But as one studies the paintings in more detail, it becomes obvious that much thought has gone into the construction of the designs. Cave painting was traditionally kept simple and uncluttered with extraneous detail, as the Aboriginal artists have a great sense of artistic composition and balance. The art of Ayers Rock must be looked at in the knowledge that it is, in essence, a pure 'stone age' art form that has developed untouched, until relatively recently, by any other culture. It is an art of unique significance and many of the abstract designs are such that no interpretation is possible either by Europeans or the Aboriginal Elders themselves. Many of the paintings are of a kind that can only be described by the artist or someone who was present at the artist's original explanation of the design.

There are many paintings to be seen around Ayers Rock. None of them are actually sacred in their own right, but many depict subjects that are sacred, such as sacred objects, sacred areas or particularly sacred ritual stories. Such paintings are consequently of special importance and may not be interpreted to casual visitors or indeed, to anyone not entitled, in the view of the Elders, to know about the subject depicted.

Generally, the paintings reflect important influences on the Aboriginal way of life. These cover the creation of the world and the ancestors of man; the relationship of man to the natural world, to the animals and the plants and also to the elements. The stories of the Dreamtime detail the forming of the earth and its geological features. Every human emotion is the subject of a myth and the myths cover all possible story forms, including those for the very young that emphasise moral responsibility, generosity, the sharing of property and the giving of assistance to those in need. Others tell of the punishments to be expected for bad behaviour, selfishness or dangerous conduct or for hatred, lust, rape and war. These dramatic tales are illustrated in the cave paintings and in song, and in this way are handed down from generation to generation.

It is regrettable that these old paintings are fading and there is no way at present of preserving them. Preservation of rock art is not only a problem in Australia, but in every country of the world that has rock paintings. Scientific authorities in Australia and other countries are endeavouring to find the answer to the problem but so far there seems to be little promise of a quick breakthrough so we must be prepared for the eventual loss of these original paintings.

Rock paintings in Fertility Cave and Mutitjula Cave. The stories of the Rock like all Aboriginal legends are the responsibility of certain men and cannot be passed on without the permission of the Aboriginal Elders concerned. Visitors to the Rock are, however, told a great deal about the stories that can be recounted with the permission of the Elders. The rock paintings are done with red and yellow ochre, white ash and charcoal — simple materials mixed with water and applied to the cave walls with the fingers. Careful appraisal of these apparently simple paintings shows the deep, underlying symbolism and economy of line necessitated by the scarceness of materials. Each and every design is complete and effective on its own but only the knowledge of the Elders enables this art to be properly interpreted.

The Mala man, the ritual ancestor of the people of Uluru. The paintings at Uluru illustrate the stories and legends of creation. These legends cover every facet of life and tell of the rewards of being good members of the community or the punishments that follow from breaking the law.

FLORA AND FAUNA

In the National Park, Ayers Rock, the mighty monolith rising starkly from the surrounding mulga and sandplains dominates the scene, and provides a broad spectrum of habitats for the creatures and plants of the desert.

During its formation in the Cambrian period, the Rock was tilted by earth movements and pressures and its strata are now almost standing on end, at 85 degrees to the horizontal. The strata runs along the top of the rock in a south-east to north-west direction and over millions of years the climate, the winds and the rains have worn the softer strata lines causing grooves, holes and pans to be formed. When it rains these holes become waterholes, very welcome to the animal life on top of the Rock. Some of the deeper and more protected holes are almost permanent, and some of these waterholes on the summit are important in the rituals of the Aboriginal people. Around the more permanent waterholes grow a wealth of plants including sedges, mosses and ferns, together with the Australian Bluebells (*Wahlenbergia spp.*) and the Rock Isotome (*Isotoma petraea*). This attractive plant has poisonous juice that can cause pain and lead to a temporary blindness if squirted into the eyes. Around the water also grow grasses such as the Weeping Lovegrasses (*Eragrostis spp.*) and *Triodia basedowii* and *Triodia irritans*. There are also larger trees of the Acacia family (*A. doratoxylon*). The permanent waterholes are well-protected in the eroded strata lines of the Rock and, with their plantlife, cool, shady conditions and sandy patches, provide a welcome resting point to visitors after the arduous climb to the summit and the walk along the top of Uluru, the mighty Rock.

The top of the Rock is the home of many animals. The euro is in his natural environment, and the rabbit lives in the nooks and crannies under and amongst the rocks. The dingo and the fox also live there, but are rarely seen.

The Rock Wallaby used to live at Ayers Rock but has now disappeared. The reason for its disappearance is not known but cats and foxes could be responsible. More knowledge is needed before this question can be resolved.

Rock figs grow well on the Rock, taking root in the minutest cracks and, over the years, have gradually forced their roots deeper and deeper, contributing to the breaking down of the Rock into the soils and sands. The figtrees attract a wealth of birdlife. The Black-faced Cuckoo Shrike particularly loves the figs and wheels around them constantly. Under the figtrees are many forms of insect life — ants, beetles, huntsman spiders and others. The jumping spiders, extremely well protected by their coloration which blends into the colour of their rock habitat, anchor themselves with a strand of their silk, and leap distances that are large compared with their size.

The eroded caves and ledges high up the walls are the nesting places and roosting spots of the Nankeen Kestrel (*Falco cenchroides*) and the Crow (*Corvus orru*). The Wedgetail Eagle (*Aquila audax*) sits there looking out over his vast domain.

Around the base of the Rock are many shallow caves and gorges. The circumference of the Rock has always been split into two ritual zones by the Aborigines of the area. One was Tjindulagul, the sun side, whilst the other was Umbaluru, the shade side, a very obvious, but most definite difference. On the sunny side, that is the north side, the waterholes are generally only full for a limited period due to the exposure to the hot sun and the high evaporation. A few small areas provide sufficient shade to prevent too drastic drying out and some good stands of bloodwoods (*Eucalyptus terminalis*), with an understorey of hopbush (*Dodonaea viscosa*), plum bush (*Santalum lanceolatum*) and a species of the hibiscus family, Abutilon (an attractive yellow hibiscus flower with moist green leaves) growing profusely in the well protected places. On the south side of the Rock which is nearly always in the shade, however, there is a great variety of dense vegetation. During most of the year, the sun only lights up the walls for a short period. It is only in August that the rising sun lights up the whole of the south side but, even then, the walls protruding from the deeper gorges quickly throw their shadows along, keeping the moist and cool conditions within the clefts.

The Black-shouldered Kite, a bird of the inland, hunts reptiles and small rodents. With its true hovering flight, and accurate attack, few of its prey escape.

All over the Rock there are black marks that are the courses followed by the rainwater. The black is an algae, of the *Calythrix* species, and at the bottom of these runs are the waterholes, some of which are quite large and deep and can be classed as almost permanent water. Maggie Springs, or, as it is known to the Aborigines, Mutidjula, is a good example of this. The growth in these cool, wet zones is heavy. The prominent grass species are *Themeda avanacea*, wild oats, and its relative, *Themeda australis*, kangaroo grass. Both these grasses are tall and stately. Their seed heads sway gently in the breezes and the sunlight shining through them gives them an almost magical quality. The figtrees and plums are abundant, as is the hopbush and the eremophila species. It is the bloodwood gum, however, that towers over all the trees and the stands of young trees are extremely thick. Among the leaf litter and grasses, near the particularly moist areas one finds the Drosera insect consuming plants, and the mosses, lichens and liverworts thrive in these conditions. The ferns are very evident under the boulders and in the cracks in the rock itself. In certain places one can find the 'trigger' plant *Stylidium inaequipetalum*, a very beautiful.little flower that is designed so that any insect entering the flower trips a delicate mechanism and is struck on the back with a pollen-loaded stamen. In another spot grows the very attractive *Gastrolobium grandiflorum*, which has wonderful flowers but, like a great many of the 'pea' plants, is extremely poisonous.

These areas are magnificent wildlife habitats and birds, reptiles and mammals abound. The Cuckoo Shrikes (*Coracina novae-hollandiae*) and Grey-headed Honeyeaters (*Meliphaga keartlandi*) are amongst the more common birds, but there is the Masked Woodswallow (*Artamus personatus*) and its fellow the Black-faced Woodswallow (*Artamus cinereus*). The Zebra Finch (*Poephila guttata*), the Diamond Dove (*Geopelia cuneata*), the Crested Pigeon (*Ocyphaps lophotes*) and many others are to be seen. The caves attract the Fairy Martins (*Petrochelidon ariel*) and many of their bottle-shaped nests are built in the caves.

The reptiles need more careful observation, but one can find poisonous snakes such as the King Brown (*Pseudechis australia*), and the Western Brown (*Pseudonaja nuchalis*) as well as the smaller snakes, such as the five-ringed or banded burrowing species. The largest lizard near the Rock is the tremendous Perentie (*Varanus giganteus*). This reptile can grow to over two metres, and is the second largest lizard in the world, after the Komodo dragon of Indonesia.The Perentie do not usually move away too rapidly, so one can often manage to photograph them. It is not, however, advisable to approach too close to this lizard as it is equipped with an efficient set of claws. Its bite could also be painful. Although Australian lizards are not poisonous, some species are well able to inflict severe bites and like all wildlife, must be treated with respect.

As in all habitats of the central Australian arid areas, the animal life becomes active at nightfall. Bats leave the cool caves where they have sheltered during the day, and other species emerge from the hollow trees where they have sought security, and go off to catch their food. Owls slowly appear and take up their lookout posts, patiently settling themselves prior to a quick and accurate plunge when their ears catch the rustling of the rodents in the scrub or on the rocks. The ordinary housemouse competes for the food with *Pseudomys hermannsburgensis*, a much more endearing rodent. The main marsupial of the immediate Rock area is the Red-eared Antechinus (*Antechinus macdonnellensis*), a fascinating animal with a great character of its own. This marsupial is a fat-tailed species and lives mostly on insects, such as beetles and moths, and also spiders and grasshoppers that fall victim to its hunting. The Antechinus appear to hunt by sound and sight, although they certainly have a good 'nose'. In captivity they have shown little interest in animals given as food until the prey moves and then they pounce very rapidly and the prey is consumed. The Antechinus shows a fondness for water and it often lives near water, although there are also populations in the drier areas.

The Red Kangaroo is an animal of the inland plains, and is generally to be found where the rainfall is less than 400 millimetres. Large male 'Reds' can exceed 90 kilograms. During adverse weather conditions kangaroos cease to breed but the female retains an embryo in the uterus until conditions are suitable.

While the Antechinus is hunting among the fallen rocks and leaf litter and the owls are wheeling through the tree canopy giving out with their shrieking calls, the euro comes out from his daytime hideout and grazes on the herbs and grasses around the Rock base. The euro has a completely different diet to the kangaroo. Whereas the kangaroo eats approximately 75 per cent grasses and herbs, the euro consumes around 75 per cent hard spinifex and the remaining portion of its diet comprises the softer grasses. The kangaroo and the euro, therefore, do not in any way compete; they normally live in completely different types of country and so do not crop the same foodplants. In this way nature has made sure there is not too much competition for food. It is unfortunately human beings, with their introduction of exotic animals, that have disturbed the balance of nature for the native Australian animals.

As night proceeds to engulf the Rock, the animals continue their food gathering, and the Children's Python (*Liasis childreni*) steals silently out from the deep rock crevasses and joins the predators in their search for prey. Eventually a glow appears on the eastern horizon, the tourist coaches begin to roar along the roads, the generators start up. The antechinus scurry back to the safety of the rocks and slowly and reluctantly the euros move back into the shade of the Rock and to their hides. Ayers Rock has once again been given back to the two-legged animal — man.

(Above right) One of the most interesting and absorbing animals to be found on Ayers Rock, the Shield Shrimp, *Triops australiensis*, is believed to have existed for over 150 million years.

(Right) More often associated with cooler climes, the Echidna lives around Ayers Rock in the cooler sections, particularly in the Maggie Springs area. It is very rarely seen but the evidence of raided termite nests shows that the animal is present in good numbers within its preferred habitat.

(Above) A frog of the Cyclorana genus, one of the water-holding species that were of tremendous importance to the old desert nomads. Living about one hundred centimetres below ground in humid burrows, these frogs are able to survive considerable periods of drought. When the rains come, the frogs very quickly make their way to the surface and greet the wet with a clamour of croaks. They breed rapidly in order to obtain full benefit from the waterholes and ensure that the tadpoles achieve adulthood before the waters dry up.

(Left) There are many interesting reptiles throughout the park but the Children's python is one of the most attractive animals that can be found. Completely harmless, it is nevertheless often mistaken for a poisonous snake and killed. If one is not able to identify snakes and pythons do not take any risks. Generally the wisest course is to allow the reptile to move away rather than attempt to kill it. Most people that have been bitten by snakes were attempting to kill or capture them.

The Red-eared Antechinus *(Antechinus macdonnell-ensis)*, a marsupial that lives among the boulders at the base of the Rock as well as on the top is an attractive animal with a great deal of character. A very efficient and quick predator, it is mainly insectivorous. Generally the females give birth to about six young and at birth these minute animals afix themselves to the teats within the pouch (which is really only a fold of skin) and are carried around in this manner until they grow big enough to hang on to the mother's back.

(*Above*) A stately bird of the outback, the Australian Bustard has been a popular food of both the Aborigines and European settlers. Now a protected species, there is sign that it is increasing its numbers once more. The feathers and bones of this bird were used by Aborigines for artifacts and ritual ornaments.

(*Right*) The Wedgetail Eagle — a magnificent bird of prey. Young birds are a rich brown with golden highlights and as they grow older their plumage becomes black. The eagle builds large nests in the fork of trees, both high Desert Oaks and low mulga species.

(*Far Right*) The Cockatiel is a nomadic bird that appears in the park area during the months of July to November at about the same time as the budgerigars. Wheeling about the sandhills in flocks of over a hundred they constitute a wonderful sight. The Cockatiels nest in hollows in dead trees as do most species of parrot.

A common butterfly of the area, the Wanderer is another name for the Monarch Butterfly of the United States of America. It lives on the Caustic milkweed *(Euphorbia spp.)* and is unpalatable to predators due to the poisonous qualities of the milkweed — another interesting defence mechanism.

(Right) Trees and plants play their part in the breaking down of the rock into soils. Here a eucalypt has been able to grow in a crack on the side of the rock. As the roots of the tree grow, pressures will be exerted on the rock and eventually a piece will break off. This continuing process can be seen in many areas of the Rock, particularly where Rock Figs are growing.

(Below) Shown here on the flower buds of the Newcastlia shrub, this Praying Mantis is another example of nature's camouflage. Harmless to man, the Mantis is a ferocious-looking insect that in fact assists mankind in the control of many species of insect.

(Left) The processional caterpillar, sometimes referred to as the 'Itchy grub', lives in this nest, leaving it at night to feed on the leaves of the host tree. Eventually they make their way down to the ground and set off in a column to find suitable soft ground in which to burrow and pupate. These nests can be seen in all types of tree in central Australia and they are one reason why one should not camp under a tree. If these nests break open, the long caterpillar hairs could get into one's eyes causing severe irritation.

(Top left) Pussycat tails, *Ptilotus macrocephalus*, growing at the base of the Rock, one of the most attractive dry region flowers. Within the park there are a number of species of these flowers, all very beautiful.

(Left) Rock isotome, a beautiful flower found in many of the park's cooler and moister areas. It should not be picked or handled as the juices get into the eyes, and cause painful irritation.

(Above) *Gastrolobium grandiflorum*, a very poisonous member of the 'pea' family. One Aboriginal legend tells of an area taboo to uninitiated people. One of the protective devices to ensure that no one has access to this area was this very dangerous plant.

THE MULGA WILDERNESS

On a warm day the Bearded Dragon basks in the sunshine on a dead tree.

The mulga is a quiet place. In the depths of a dense stand of mulga (*Acacia aneura*) there is a very great sense of solitude. The trees cut off the breeze and with the sun beating down during the heat of the day, very few animals leave the relative comfort of their burrows or the shade of the trees.

Among the trees, the Singing Honeyeater (*Meliphaga virescens*) can be heard gently sending out its call. The Thornbills, Chestnut-rumped (*Acanthiza uropygialis*) and Yellow-tailed (*A. chrysorrhoa*) flit about in the cool shade. Mulga parrots (*Psephotus varius*) can be seen resting up in the thicker growth of the mulga, whilst the Willie Wagtail (*Rhipidura leucophrys*) flies rapidly out from cover to catch a tempting insect on the wing. On the top of dead trees, the Brown Hawks (*Falco berigora*) and the Nankeen Kestrel (*Falco cenchroides*) wait for their prey.

Lizards of the Dragon family warm themselves by basking on the dead limbs of fallen, or even on standing dead trees. Approach them and you will notice the rapid cocking of the eye and the gentle movement away from you, around the branch. Move closer still and the lizard drops immediately to the ground and darts for his bolthole, there to await the passing of the obvious danger.

As the day wears on, a Plains turkey (*Eupodotis australis*) will possibly walk stately by; it does not appear to be quite as affected by the heat as other birds. It saunters casually past and does not appear to be overly concerned at the presence of humans. That is until some overt movement is made and, with a great and laborious flapping of the heavy wings, *kipara*, the turkey flies off to safety.

As the mulga area cools and the shadows lengthen the animals and birds come to life. A rustle in the leaf litter under the trees announces the arrival of the rodents, maybe *Mus musculus*, the ubiquitous domestic mouse that is found throughout the region. Perhaps *Pseudomys hermannsburgensis*, an attractive native rodent, or even the Long-haired Rat, sometimes known as the Plague rat (*Rattus villosissimus*). This animal derives its name 'Plague' from the way in which its population sometimes explodes and rapidly extends over thousands of square kilometres of country. The first appearance of this rat in the park was recorded in 1975. Animals, including breeding females, were captured and, although their population did not reach plague proportions, there were a considerable number of them in the area.

Yet other disturbances in the leaf litter could be caused by the King Brown Snake (*Pseudechis australis*), the largest poisonous snake of the park. These snakes may grow up to 240 centimetres in length, and are most definitely to be respected.

The beautiful wrens, the Turquoise Wren (*Malurus callainus*) and the White-winged Wren (*M. leuconotus*) flit about the undergrowth keeping up a constant calling to each other. The wrens are probably the most attractive family in the mulga environment.

Old man kangaroo (*Megaleia rufa*), the Big Red Kangaroo and his mate, the Blue Flier, move out from the mulga trees where they have spent most of the day, keeping themselves cool by constantly licking their wrists in order to lower blood temperature. Passers-by would probably miss seeing them altogether, unless they happened to catch the flick of an ear, now and again.

As night time approaches, the skinks, such as *Ctenotus pantherinus*, can be seen nosing about the tree debris for their evening meal. Moths and beetles fly here and there and, in a final burst of energy, the small bush birds like the Hooded and Redcapped Robins (*Petroica cucullata*, and *P. goodenovii*) make their flying captures extremely efficiently. The predator birds, the Brown Hawk and the Kestrels, manage to take their prey before dark and then move off to roost and leave the field to the night birds, the Frogmouth (*Podargus strigoides*), the Boobook owl (*Ninox novaeseelandiae*), the Barn owl (*Tyto alba*) and the Spotted Nightjar (*Eurostopodus guttatus*).

The Perentie, the second largest lizard in the world, is only surpassed by the Komodo dragon of Indonesia, a beautiful reptile that is a much-enjoyed delicacy of the Aboriginal people. Although capable of moving fast the perentie is generally quite slow and confident and is therefore easy to hunt and kill. It lays a number of eggs in deep burrows. These eggs are also a popular food of the Aborigines.

As darkness takes over, the carnivorous marsupials appear, small animals which are some of the most attractive creatures of Australian wildlife. Two species of Sminthopsis, or marsupial mice, associated with the mulga zone, *Sminthopsis ooldea*, and *Sminthopsis froggatti*, are easily confused as both are relatively long-tailed species. The *S. froggatti*, however, have a very marked black head stripe, which shows between their eyes and extends over their foreheads; this stripe gives the common name — Stripe-headed marsupial mouse. The other species associated with the mulga, but particularly where stony ground intrudes, is the fat-tailed marsupial mouse, *Sminthopsis crassicaudatus* — meaning fat tail. This mouse cannot be confused with others as its tail is almost carrot-shaped and shorter than its head and body. The coloration of these interesting animals is a drab grey, marked with lighter underbellies and darker body hairs. These small and secretive animals live in shallow burrows or inside dead mulga branches. The manner in which they conceal themselves makes them extremely difficult to see for any but the most observant.

The Sminthopsis family are extremely efficient predators and play their part in the control of insect and rodent life. In turn they provide prey for larger predators such as dingoes, foxes, hawks and owls.

Night continues and the nocturnal geckoes, like the Spiny-Tailed Gecko hunts his insect food and is himself hunted. Slowly dawn draws near and, with the rising of the sun, activity increases and then, once again, subsides as the mulga becomes hotter and hotter and life becomes still and silent beneath the acacia cover.

At first sight plantlife amongst the mulga appears to consist only of thorns and prickly burrs. Normally, the growth appears grey and drab; wispy grass is interspersed with the mulga. A few Parakeelya (*Calandrinia spp.*) remain from the last rains, and a number of withered stems of daisies, such as *Senecio gregorii* or *Minuria leptophylla* may also have survived. Eremophila shrubs, particularly the *Eremophila latrobei* and *Eremophila alternifolia* are scattered throughout the trees but, generally, although the mulga woodland has a great many interesting flora species, the overall impression is one of dryness and death. Dead trees stand or lie all over the place, the leaf litter and, of course, seeds gather under and alongside the fallen timber. Walking through mulga can very easily result in a staked leg, and any wound caused by mulga should be disinfected as it can turn extremely septic very quickly. It is with the rains that the flora of the mulga area appear in a magnificent array.

(Top right) An example of the fantastic camouflage to be found in nature is this Spiny-Tailed Gecko on a fallen tree. This camouflage is only one of this reptile's defensive mechanisms; its tailspines, from which it gets its common name, can exude a strong-smelling substance.

(Right) One of the more attractive reptiles of the mulga region, the bright colouration of this delicate lizard, the Diporiphora Dragon, catches the eye in the generally drab grey mulga.

(Above) In the dry periods vegetation in the mulga dries out, breaks up and is blown away. As periods of drought continue large tracts of land eventually become completely bare. At times like these all animal life slows down and awaits the breaking of the drought.

(Right) Following the wet periods which induce high, lush vegetation, the danger of fire arises. Usually started by lightning strikes, the fires rage through the spinifex-covered sandhills and the mulga scrub. Fire ecology is a relatively new study but it seems that both hot summer fires and slower 'cooler' winter fires that are experienced periodically ensure vigorous plant growth.

(Top, far right) A 'hot' fire passing through mulga can completely denude the area. Nesting birds face high mortality but most reptiles and mammals seem to be able to avoid death by their living in burrows.

(Far right) Remarkably soon after fire and especially following good rains, new growth appears on the barren ground. The ash and charcoal from the fires provide a fertiliser and the lightning that was responsible for the fires also benefits the plants. A flash of lightning splits up nitrogen molecules and causes a reaction that forms calcium nitrates, a much-needed element in desert soils that are usually nitrogen deficient.

(Top) The beautiful flowers of the various mistletoes are a great attraction to a number of birds, especially the small attractive Mistletoe bird. Insects also are attracted by the blooms and so the lowly mistletoe plays its part in the chain of life.

(Middle) Throughout the mulga areas there are rock outcrops or breakaway country. A slight vegetation change is apparent but most plant species are closely related to those in the mulga. In these outcrop areas strong animal populations are to be found and they are of great interest to naturalists.

(Right) A typical mulga scene sometime after rain. Clumps of small white daisies cover the ground between the trees. Attracting many insects the daisies also provide protection and cover for many of the small inhabitants of the mulga.

(Far right) After a period of rain the grasses and herbs of the mulga zone attract the kangaroos, who find the vegetation of the mulga wilderness much more to their liking than the grasses of the sandplains. The soft grasses and herbs that are usually found growing on the clay soils of the mulga environment make up about 75 per cent of the kangaroos' diet.

(Top) The Western Brown Snake shown here in the mulga, can be found throughout the park. It is one of the two most dangerous snakes in the area, the other being the King Brown Snake. It is wise to avoid these reptiles and no attempt should be made to catch or kill snakes unless they happen to move into one's camp and there is no alternative.

(Right) The Red-capped Robin is one of the many highly coloured and beautiful birds of the area and one that is particularly associated with mulga. This bird has little fear of man and is quite inquisitive. The male and female share the nest building and the feeding of their young. The nest is a beautifully designed cup usually placed in the fork of a dead tree relatively close to the ground.

(Top, far right) A marsupial mouse that lives in the mulga areas, the *Sminthopsis ooldea* usually lives in a hollow log or branch. Whilst it sometimes kills other small mammals it is normally described as insectivorous. The name *Sminthopsis* is of the Greek origin and means 'hedgehoglike'. The species name *ooldea* is taken from the Aboriginal name for a waterhole which lies on the route of the Transcontinental railway in the place where Daisy Bates lived among the Aboriginal people.

(Left) While not as glorious in colour as its male counterpart, the female Turquoise Wren nevertheless has a beauty of her own. They are active all day constantly hunting and moving around the low shrubs. When young are in the nest, not only the parents but also all members of the group, assist in the feeding.

(Right) The male Turquoise Wren is one of the most beautiful of all Australian birds. Active and gregarious, it shows little fear of humans. The male bird plays a full part in the brooding of the eggs and the feeding of the young.

SANDHILLS AND SANDPLAINS

On the sandhills and the sandplains the Acacias flower profusely with the coming of the winter rains. Aborigines have made use of the water the Acacias store in their roots.

In leaving the mulga stands, one enters the sandhills and sandplains, where the sparse vegetation stands out in dramatic contrast to the deep red soil. Some of the dunes rise fifteen to twenty metres from the plains. Everything appears much more inviting than in the mulga wilderness, although the same hot sun beats down with the same intensity. The breeze appears stronger and the heat feels a little less oppressive.

The spinifex (*Triodia basedowii*) dominated plains stretch far into the distance, the mulga protruding here and there. There are two types of spinifex, generally referred to as hard and soft. The tremendous sandplain tree, the Desert Oak (*Casuarina decaisneana*), shows out in magnificent stands, whilst the Grevilleas (*juncifolia, eriostachya* and *stenobotrya*) dominate the sandhill crests and interdune swales. The Grevilleas are among the most brilliant of the sand country flora, and *G. eriostachya* is a popular food plant for the Aborigines. A sweet, honey-like nectar is produced and the Aborigines delight in this, as do the varied honeyeaters that inhabit this area: the Singing Honeyeater (*Meliphaga virescens*), the Spiny-cheeked Honeyeater (*Anthochaera rufogularis*), the Black Honeyeater (*Myzomela nigra*), the White-plumed Honeyeater (*Meliphaga pencillata*) and the Pied Honeyeater (*Certhionyx variegatus*).

Despite the fact that there is almost no nutrient value in the red sand, a great variety of wonderful plants live on the sandhill crests. There are lovely plants such as the rattlepods *Crotelaria cunninghamii* and *C. strehlowii*, together with *Eremophila christopherii* and a variety of small and delicate 'pea' plants.

Gyrostemon ramulosas is an outstanding small tree living almost solely on the sandhills and is a relative of the Desert Poplar (*Codonocarpus continifolius*) that grows in good periods throughout the swales. Between the sand dunes and up the sand slopes are the Thryptomenes and the Baeckeas, both impressively pretty, small shrubs that are popular as garden plants. *Thryptomene maisonneuvii* is another plant at one time used by the Aborigines, the fresh dew from the plant providing a sweet, sugary drink. The extremely beautiful and delicate Desert Myrtle (*Calytrix longiflora*) with its flowers of subdued pastel tints grows here among the spinifex plants.

The animal life is as varied and as interesting as the flora. Even during the hottest part of the day, the small Military Dragon can be seen. An attractive reptile with bright red, black and yellow coloration, its very long rear legs stretch well in front of its head, thereby permitting movement at great speed. When disturbed, it's away into the Triodia, and intending capturers risk a nose-full or hand-full of porcupine grass.

Along with the Military Dragon, reptile life in the sandhills is profuse. There can be found the Woma or sandhill python (*Aspidites ramsayi*), the King Brown and Western Brown Snakes. A number of the small burrowing snakes such as the Simoselaps species are also there, as are the legless lizards and Two-toed Desert Skinks; the Sand Goanna (*Varanus gouldii*), the Western Skink (*Tiliqua occipitalis*) and Centralian Bluetongue Skink (T. multifasciatus); the *Egernia kintorei* lizard that lives in an extensive burrow in the sandhills and can bite like a vice. The sand dunes are full of life.

One of the most fascinating reptiles is the Thorny Devil (*Moloch horridus*) which, despite its prickly appearance, is completely harmless. Living exclusively on a diet of small ants, this lizard is often taken by people as a pet, without them realising that they are condemning it to a slow death by starvation. This lizard drinks in a wonderful way, the skin soaking up water from the shallowest pool or the lightest shower, which then finds its way by capillary action to the reptile's mouth.

Under the Desert Oaks is a cool, somewhat temperate zone. The red sand is insulated by the carpet of needlelike leaf litter of the tree, and this is the habitat of the Inch ant, a brown and black insect measuring a length of one inch (2.4 centimetres) — hence the name. This ant (*Myrmecia spp.*) is primitive and ferocious, and attacks with little provocation. The burning bite of these small creatures is very painful and, after the initial pain subsides, irritation continues in the form of an itch. The ants and the bushflies that are persistent and annoying when attracted to the perspiration on one's face, were well known to the early explorers. Ernest Giles mentioned them in his journals. After losing his man Gibson, in the desert that now bears his name, Giles had to walk carrying his water barrel, continually annoyed by the flies and noting that he was unable to rest in the shade of the Oaks because of the 'bull ants'.

The camel was brought to Australia for use as beast of burden by explorers. Some escaped and others were released after exploring trips and bred successfully in the arid zones. There are now hundreds in the sandplain country that surrounds the park. Like most imported animals the camel has an effect on the native flora and fauna. They are capable of causing changes to vegetation and it has been suggested that the Quandong is being eaten out in many areas. There has not yet been a definitive study of the camel and little control work is being done.

Throughout the sandplains, the tracks of camels are regularly seen. There are hundreds of camels in the saltpan areas bordering the park, and they often pass through or visit when weather conditions are right. Most of their movement takes place at night, which is also the time for most of the mammal activity in the dunes.

Another member of the Sminthopsis family, the *S. hirtipes*, lives on the dune tops. This very attractively coloured animal with a golden brown back, white underneath and white fringes over its feet, from which comes the name *hirtipes*, literally hairy feet. Sminthopsis means 'hedgehog like', as a reference to the grey and black animals of the mulga appearing almost spiky to the casual observer. *S. hirtipes* was caught in the park in late 1975 for the first time on record in the Northern Territory since the Horn Expedition in 1896.

Also on top of the dunes lives one of the most popular and engaging desert creatures — the Hopping Mouse (*Notomys alexis*), sometimes known as the Kangaroo Mouse. As these are not marsupial creatures, Hopping Mouse is perhaps the better name. During periods of population explosion, the mice visit campsites and houses and will cheekily take food from the hand. When the population density has reached its limit, *Notomys* stop breeding. Parasites eventually attack the animals and the population diminishes as quickly as it grew.

In the interdune swales, the burrows of the Mulgara, (*Dasycercus cristicauda*), or Crest-tailed marsupial mouse, can be found. The burrows are shallow, but complex, with a number of corridors and nesting places. The Mulgara is an engaging marsupial; intelligent and quick of action it shows a great character. The Mulgara is able to live on a carnivorous diet without need for separate water, as it has a most efficient kidney system that keeps moisture loss to a minimum.

Somewhere within the sandhill complex lives the secretive Marsupial Mole (*Notorcytes typhlops*), a small golden animal with a horny shield on the nose, a tiny ringed tail and the usual molelike digging claws. As there is still very little known about this mole, it is to be hoped that more animals can be found in order to add to the knowledge of this very interesting desert creature. Recent records of a mole within the park include one that was killed by an Aborigine's hunting dog in 1974 and in March 1978 a live one was found near the Sunset viewing area. The animal was photographed and released.

As in all areas of the park, insect life is profuse; on the sandhills, tiny ants and trapdoor spiders are to be found, together with many forms of beetles and moths and butterflies. An early morning visit to a dune crest will illustrate, to those interested, the drama of life played out during the hours of darkness.

(Right) An attractive desert tree, the Desert Oak *(Casuarina decaisencana)*. Its value to the arid region of Central Australia is not yet fully understood, but it is not difficult to appreciate the local importance of the cool shade area to many forms of animal life. The ground is covered sometimes to a depth of ten centimetres by fallen leaf needles.

(Next page) Looking out from a sandhill one has a view that crosses many kilometres of sandhill and sandplain country. Dominant trees are the Desert Oaks whilst the Triodia grasses known as spinifex cover the whole area.

(Top, far left) One of the attractive sandplain flora *Newcastlia spodiotricha* has only its beauty to offer. When in flower, it is very attractive to the native bees and wasps, and a plant in full bloom constantly hums with the attention of many insects. Close observation will often show a number of dragon lizards, predators on the insects.

(Far Left) Baeckea polystemona, a small, delicate, waxlike flower with minute leaves, is to be found on the sandplains.

The Centralian Bluetongue Skink *(Middle left)* and the Western Bluetongue skink *(Above)* meet at Uluru National park. They are identified by the colour and size of the body bands. Both these reptiles are a popular food animal of the Aborigines.

(Left) The Knob-tailed Gecko, an attractive nocturnal gecko that lives in a small burrow. Little is known of its habits except that it hunts at night in the open spaces. This gecko is the *Nephurus Levis*, one of three species of Nephurus to be found in the park area.

(Top) The Marsupial Mole, one of the most remarkable and specialised animals of the Centre. Little is known of the life or habits of this mole and very few specimens have been caught. This is one of very few photographs in existence. This mole was caught at Ayers Rock near the sunset viewing dune by two park rangers Ian Marshall and Dennis Matthews and after it was photographed it was released at the point of capture. So little is known of its food-type, the required quantity of food or the length of time the animal could do without it that it was considered dangerous to keep it in captivity. The mole, *Itjaritjari* in the Pitjantjatjara language, is also a significant Dreamtime creature who was a peaceful, kind ancestor.

(Above) One of the sandplains' most fascinating inhabitants the Mulgara (also known as Cannings' little dog) is a shy, nocturnal animal. It is an efficient carnivore and plays an important part in the control of rodents. During good seasons it is fairly common but still difficult to see because of its shy nature. It likes to bask in the sunshine during the cooler, winter days.

(Right) The White-fronted Honeyeater, a nomadic honeyeater that nests in low shrubs in the sandplain areas. A shy, beautifully coloured bird, it lives on the nectar of the sandhill flora.

(Top) Living in deep burrows in the sand, the scorpion emerges when moist air promises rain. The scorpion of the centre is not considered dangerous although the sting is painful.

(Above) Cunningham's Rattlepod, a member of the 'pea' family that grows on the crests of the sandhills, is commonly called 'Parrot flower' or 'Carnarvon Bird' flower. Despite the magnificence of its flower, it is another poisonous plant. There are probably few flowers that can surpass this rattlepod for beauty.

(Right) A fearsome looking yet harmless reptile that lives in the sandplains, the Thorny Devil exists by eating a type of small ant and a meal can consist of over 3,000 ants.

THE OLGAS

The setting sun silhouettes the Olgas group and lights the spinifex-covered sandplains and mulga scrubland. Although these Triodia grasses are referred to as spinifex, true spinifex is a soft coastal grass whilst Triodia well illustrates its common name, 'porcupine grass'.

The magnificent domes known as the Olgas are situated 32 kilometres west of Ayers Rock. The group of over thirty domes fascinates many visitors today in the same way that it has fascinated the Aboriginal people during the thousands of years they have inhabited the region.

It also worked its magic on the first European man to see it, the explorer Ernest Giles, who gave the name Mount Olga to its highest dome. Giles wrote in his journals after he had finally visited both Ayers Rock and Mount Olga,

> The appearance of Mount Olga from this camp is truly wonderful; it displayed to our astonished eyes, rounded minarets, giant cupolas and monstrous domes. There they have stood as huge memorials from the ancient times of earth, for ages, countless eons of ages since creation first had birth ... Mount Olga is the more wonderful and grotesque; Mount Ayers the more ancient and sublime.

In this final sentence, Giles has summed up the feelings of the Aboriginal people to both these beautiful symbols of the Dreamtime.

Within the cool gorges of the Olgas, moisture is retained for considerable periods after rain, although there are no permanent waterholes. Plant and animal life naturally flourish within these cooler areas and visitors also relish the relief to be experienced as a contrast to the hot, dusty sandplains that surround Mount Olga. The area covered by the domes and gorges of the Olgas offers a large fascinating wilderness where enjoyment can be found in long walks, climbing, wildlife observation and photography or just resting in the shade.

Many of the domes are suitable for free climbing but it must be understood that they can be dangerous and the inexperienced should only climb marked routes such as are available in the Valley of the Winds and the Katatjuta look-out gorge. Both these climbs are suitable for family enjoyment and after the walk comes the reward of breathtaking views over some of the most beautiful country in central Australia.

Mount Olga, itself, stands 546 metres above the plains and 1072 metres above sea level. Half as high again as Ayers Rock, it is a very demanding climb that should be treated with caution. The Olga Gorge, known to the Aborigines as *Walpa* meaning 'windy', is also a very interesting climb through to the central valley of the Olga group. This route is not for the inexperienced or unfit bushwalker but is most definitely worth the effort for any keen naturalist. Within the narrowing cleft are to be found varied interesting plants, whilst birdlife is usually prolific. The Chiming Wedgebill, a bird which is not seen often, is to be found in this area.

Climbing over and under large conglomerate boulders, eventually brings its reward when the valley opens up. Down the valley is an old Aboriginal path that leads to the Valley of the Winds. This path meanders along the banks of watercourses and waterholes that in the time of rain are very inviting on a hot day. When these watercourses are running the valley of the Olgas takes on a completely new aspect. However, they are extremely short-lived streams and are quickly absorbed by the normally parched desert sands that surround the Olgas. Information on walks and climbing can be obtained from the park ranger staff and all those who wish to experience the solitude to be found in the Olgas should get details of conditions within the Olgas before they start out.

Every feature or mark on the domes of the Olgas are evidence of the Aborigines' Dreamtime adventures and there are numerous stories and legends associated with 'Katatjuta'. As each and every story is the responsibility of certain men, and the telling of those stories is dependent on many factors, they cannot be retold in this book. However, when visitors sit in the shade of the gorges their understanding will certainly increase of the Aborigines' feeling for their country. They should also remember the beauty of the sunset on the main domes of the Olgas; a sight just as attractive and rewarding as the sunset on the Rock and a fitting end to a wonderful Olgas interlude.

The late afternoon sun shines on the southern face of Mount Olga. The contrast of sun and overcast sky reacts to produce a fascinating quality of light that is yet another example of the magnificent colour variations that are synonomous with the Rock and the Olgas.

(Left) The rain running off the bare domes of the Olgas and floods along the many creeks and watercourses that wind through the gorges within the Olga area. Eventually it floods out onto the surrounding plains ensuring a strong and lush vegetation that is able to withstand all but the severest drought.

(Top) The lines of trees and shrubs follow the edges of the Olga domes where moisture is retained the longest. Among the eroded rocks on the top of the domes grow many plants, each playing its part in the breaking down of these rocks into the soils of the desert. On the surrounding plain can be seen the taller, drab acacias and the flowering cassias.

(Above) As one approaches the Olgas, the vegetation becomes stronger and more varied. Here the eucalypts such as the 'bloodwood' become more evident and as one moves into the watercourses of the Olgas the River Red Gums can be seen.

(Top) This cliff face, sometimes referred to as 'the painted cliff', faces south and consequently the cool, shady conditions that remain constant throughout the year permit a growth of lichens. The black stains on the cliff are an algae that grows on the sections where the rainwater cascades down the cliff.

(Above) After sufficient rain, wildflowers appear in masses. Here a carpet of tiny everlasting daisies, a species of Minuria, ensures a build up of seeds and smaller protective flora that will remain dormant for many years as the cycles of nature continue.

(Right) The Valley of the Winds, one of the most popular places within the Olgas. A walk of four kilometres is rewarded by this fantastic view over the central valley of the Olgas. There are many places of interest to attract the naturalist or bushwalker but intending hikers should ensure that details of their intended route are left with someone before departing.

PETROGLYPHS AND STONE ARRANGEMENTS

At the Olgas there is only one small site where there are rock paintings as the rock surface is unsuitable for this art form. There are, however, more examples of petroglyphs or chipping of rock surfaces. The designs are pecked out on the rocks by the fracturing of the rocks' patina and usually the designs are of geometric shapes, circles, triangles and squares. There are also many animal tracks, some of the more common being the tracks of the emu, the heron, the kangaroo and the wallaby as well as those of snakes and lizards. Although only a limited number of designs are used compared with cave paintings, they are still symbolic and illustrate the spiritual life.

The Aborigines of today do not believe these designs on stone to be the work of man but believe them to have been created in the Dreamtime by the Spirit Ancestors. It has therefore been suggested that these peckings predate the ancestors of the Aborigines in the area today, and may have been the work of the first wave of Aborigines who passed through Central Australia towards the south. There is no real evidence to prove this but the present Elders definitely do not accept the petroglyphs as the work of man.

In addition to the petroglyphs there are stone arrangement sites, where, in some cases, complex geometrical designs are made up by the positioning of individual stones. These are also not accepted by the Aborigines as the work of man. There is no certain interpretation of the use of the sites. It has been suggested that they were used as a stage for the illustration of myths from a country some distance away that would not be visited by the people of this area. Usually the sites are adjacent to waterholes or soakages where nomads would rest; they could have been used to illustrate myths in order to teach and to entertain in a most inhospitable region.

During the thousands of years that these stone designs have existed, animals such as kangaroos, euros and even, later, camels have displaced some of the stones. As tourism increases, people cause more accidental movement, since in many cases they just do not notice the designs. Park authorities are aware of the problem and are endeavouring to educate the visitors to realise the importance of the stone arrangements, the petroglyphs and the cave paintings. The majority of visitors are keen to assist in preserving these art forms and thus there is some hope for the future.

(Left) Usually stone arrangements and engraving sites are found near waterholes and were presumably made whilst nomads rested near the water. There can be little doubt that the arrangements and engraved designs were used to illustrate stories of the past as the telling of stories was and still is a major part of the Aboriginal people's lives.

(Inset, next page) Throughout the Olgas stone arrangements can be found. The role that these arrangements played in the ritual life of the Aborigines is not clearly understood. Aborigines claim that these arrangements were here long before the coming of man and that they are the work of the Spirits of the Dreamtime.

(Next page) Tjuringa design — the concentric circles are the most significant design in the art of the Aborigines. Interpreted in many ways, such as place of origin, home, waterholes, breasts of women, etc., all are symbolic of creation and the cycle of life. The majority of designs engraved on rocks throughout the Olgas consist of geometric designs (circles, triangles and rhomboids) and the tracks of mammals, birds and reptiles. Many are indications of hunting areas, or waterholes but not very many can be interpreted.

FLORA AND FAUNA

Throughout the relatively cool, shaded valleys and gorges which are protected by the towering cliffs of the Olgas, live many species of native plants that are not found anywhere else within the park.

There are also colonies of reptiles that appear to live only in this environment. It is even possible that there still may be a few species of animals not yet described by wildlife scientists and so the environment of the Olgas is of great interest.

Clinging close to the rock scree slopes of the domes is a grass known only by its Latin scientific name, *Eriachne schleranthoides*. This grass is unique to the Mount Currie conglomerate and is to be found only at the Olgas and at Mount Currie itself, an outcrop some 40 kilometres west of Mount Olga. The *Eriachne* is a prickly, shrub-like grass clump, which produces some minute pea-like flowers for a short period which are extremely attractive. The flowers fade rapidly and the grass reverts to its usual, somewhat dried appearance and continues its role of providing sanctuary for the small reptiles, such as the Earless Dragon (*Tympanocryptus lineatus*), insects and small mammals, the ordinary housemouse and the native field mouse (*Pseudomys hermannsburgensis*).

Higher up the gorges in the particularly well-protected places grows the 'spearbush' (*Pandorea doratoxylon*), a very attractive vinelike plant which produces showy cream-coloured flowers, striped with mauve. Another attractive bloom is that of the mintbush (*Prostanthera striatiflora*). The flowers of this shrub are white, but also are most attractively striped with purple. This flower is sometimes referred to as 'Jockey's cap' which is a very apt name. The smell of the mintbush certainly lives up to expectations.

Sitting quietly on the rocks near one of the watercourses in the Olgas will reward the interested onlooker with the sight of many creatures. The Western Bowerbirds (*Chlamydera maculata*) may fly overhead giving out with their somewhat raucous call. They could well be on the way to their bower, so watch carefully. The Goshawk (*Accipiter fasciatus*) may come to the water to drink and most certainly the Grey-headed Honeyeaters (*Meliphaga keartlandii*) will be seen sporting themselves in the River Red Gums (*Eucalyptus camaldulensis*). In this environment, as in all others, the Willie Wagtail (*Rhipidura leucophrys*) will be around and amongst the grasses and daisies the careful observer will see small skinks and a number of dragon lizards. Some of the species that may be seen are *Tiliqua branchialis* and *Lophognathus longirostris*, a very attractive dragon with a slightly keeled back and distinctive white stripes along its sides, contrasting with its overall grey colour. The most obvious features are the extremely long tail and, when disturbed, the manner in which this reptile raises himself up on to his hind legs and runs away.

Remain quiet, and you may see snakes such as the Western Brown Snake (*Pseudonaja nuchalis*) or the Yellow-faced Whip Snake (*Demansia psammophis*). These snakes are a little dangerous, but routine care will ensure no real problem. Watch carefully and do not attempt to touch. Snakes do not generally attack humans; if permitted, they will usually move off silently.

Not to be confused with snakes are the legless lizards (*Lialis burtonis*) and scalyfoots (*Pypopus spp.*). These fascinating reptiles abound throughout the cooler and damper areas and are absolutely harmless, living on a diet of insects and small reptiles. Unfortunately, they are often mistaken for snakes and, accordingly, pay the price. It is to be hoped that people will soon accept that even snakes are important in nature and have a very important part in the ecological balance. They should only be killed if anyone is in real danger of being attacked.

Around the gorges in the Olgas appears another flower of particular interest, as it only grows at the Olgas. This beautiful flower is the Early Nancy (*Anguillaria dioica*), a lily, related to the Grasstree, or Yucca. Early Nancy only flowers in certain years and when it does flower, it is a gorgeous sight, producing a mat of pink along the watercourses. Verbene grows profusely throughout the valleys and attracts many of the insects and birds, as do the many beautiful pea species. *Hibbertia glaberimma*, an attractive yellow flower with glossy green leaves, sometimes called Guinea flower, sticks to the particularly well-shaded places, whilst throughout the valley floors are thick stands of *Acacia doratoxylon*, a very attractive wattle, especially when in bloom. *Acacia strongylophylla* with its tremendous yellow wattle flowers, and the Native Hopbush, *Dodonaea viscosa*, which also grows at the Rock, both deserve a mention. The native plum is also found here, as is the Rock fig.

The Port Lincoln Parrot (*Barnardius zonarius*) flies through the Red River Gums, calling in its bell-like tones. The Pied Butcherbird (*Cracticus nigrogularis*) is very tame and delights in sharing visitors'

The flowers of the Corkwood trees are full of nectar and used to be used by the Aborigines to make a sweet drink. The seedpods of the corkwood, shown here developing, become woody cases that eventually split open, distributing their seeds that are able to remain dormant for many years, waiting the optimum time for germination.

sandwiches. Whilst you sit enjoying your meal and pot of billy tea, keep an eye open for the Euro, who is beautifully camouflaged against the rocks. Glance at the sky and you will doubtless see the magnificent Wedgetail eagle, a bird of all habitats but particularly of the Olgas, gliding high above the tallest dome. Freckled monitors (*Varanus tristis*) silently move in the trees, attempting to catch a succulent Thornbill or Sittella. In the distance you will hear the call of the Crested Bellbird (*Oreoica gutturalis*) singing out *Pimpan panella*, *Pimpan panella* — the name of this bird in the Pitjantjatjara language.

Looking at the steep-sided cliffs, the colours catch the eye. The brown and grey of the rock, contrastiang with the black algae marks on the water areas, the green, reds and oranges of the lichens on the shaded southerly walls and the whites of a mineral exudation from sections of the rock.

The eye follows the marks of the rainwater down the walls and along the watercourses where the Droseras, with their tall and sticky leaves, which are coated with an efficient adhesive, capture myriad of tiny insects and even larger species, such as the Wanderer butterfly. Once caught there is no escape and, slowly but very efficiently, the plant extracts nitrogen from the body of its victim.

For the observant visitor the Olgas are, indeed, a fascinating place. One of the interesting aspects is the use of camouflage in nature. Look carefully on the rocky slopes and scree; the grasshoppers and small lizards are so close to the colour of the background rocks as to be almost unbelievable. The mistletoe in the gumtrees even takes on the leaf form of the host, whilst other forms of mistletoe also appear in trees such as the Mulga, with very close leaf form to that of the host plant. There are, of course, a few exceptions, but look closely and you will see the magic of nature.

Whilst looking at the mistletoes, one may see the Tawny Frogmouth (*Podargus strigoides*) sitting very, very still on a dead tree branch and appearing just like a dead and broken limb of the tree. The frogmouth could almost be the classic camouflage of the central Australian bush.

Throughout the Olga valleys can be found tiny areas representing all types of environmental conditions. Along the watercourses, beneath the overhanging ferns, and Droseras, are tiny patches of vivid green moss, liverworts and lichens. Around the edges of these watercourses, the glossy blue and spectacular red dragonflies hawk their prey. In the pools swim tadpoles. Their underwater enemy, the Water scorpion, fixes a tadpole with his pincers and inserting a long hypodermic probe, sucks the juices from his victim, discarding the remains. The Caddis fly and dragonfly larvae move about the pebbles on the bottom of the pools. The Caddis fly larvae are another example of camouflage, building for themselves a casing of tiny twigs and grains of sand, they appear just like tiny broken pieces of twig being gently moved along by water action.

As night falls, a burst of activity is evident as the reptiles take advantage of the warmth before the rapid cooling of the rocks. A few of the small marsupials appear, such as the Red-eared Antechinus, which lives here as well as at the Rock. The predators begin to arrive for the night's hunting. The dingo stalks silently through the valley and perhaps disturbs the feral cat or fox as they are about to make a kill. There is some evidence that the dingo occasionally even kills a cat for a meal whilst, at times, the Wedgetail Eagle is also predatory on them. Generally, however, the cat has no natural enemy and this makes its danger extremely obvious. The rapid population build up could only be controlled through biological methods. It appears that the cat is, at certain times, attacked by an intestinal parasite and it may be that a natural control will develop in this form.

As the night falls, the owls arrive on the scene. By their activities, the populations of the rodents and small marsupials are kept well in check. The pellets thrown up by the birds — the more indigestible parts of the prey animals, such as fur, bones and, very importantly, the skulls — are of great significance to naturalists and scientists. Over a period of time they can be used to adduce the probable numbers and the time of greatest increases and decreases in population of different types of animals.

Throughout the night, here in the Olgas as on the sandhills, in the mulga wilderness and at Ayers Rock, the drama of life continues. Nature's controls of prey and predator still interact with the climate, the changing seasons and with each other.

Found along watercourses and throughout the Olga gorges, Sturt's Desert Rose is the floral emblem of the Northern Territory.

(Top) Found throughout the park, the Black-throated Butcherbird is particularly quiet and friendly at the Olgas. A beautiful songbird, its tone has been described as the purest of any songbird. The name Butcherbird stems from the habit this bird has of hanging its prey on a spike to facilitate the eating of the flesh.

(Above) Throughout the varied habitats of the park, many spiders are to be found, from the large golden web spiders of the Nephila species to the small jumping spiders on the Rock itself. Hunters and Wolf spiders can be seen in the evening between the tussocks of spinifex. In the stalks of the spinifex this colourful member of the Argiope genus can be seen.

(Right) The Red-backed Kingfisher, a common bird during the winter months when it arrives to breed in the park. It constructs its nesting hole in the bank of a watercourse or on roadside mounds of earth and lays three to five eggs.

(Above) Following the heavy rains which cause many pools to be formed on the gravel roads of the area, many species of duck can be seen. Normally these Grey Teals would be on the more permanent waterholes in the Petermann and Musgrave ranges and along the Finke River but the widespread rains permit them to move from area to area.

(Right) One of the many acacias that cover the park, this *Acacia inequilatera* with its golden wattle flowers on red stems is very colourful.

(Above) One of a number of species of parrot to be seen in the park, the Port Lincoln Parrot is easily identified by its irridescent greens and its yellow collar. This bird is shown at its nesting hole in the trunk of a River Red Gum. This nesting hole has probably been used by the same birds, every year for the past ten years.

(Next page) Freckled Monitors can be found in all the varied habitats of the park. Here a pair preparing to mate on the top of a typical Olga conglomerate boulder. These monitors are tree climbers and very fast and efficient hunters of insects and small reptiles and mammals.